Bugs on a Log

By Debbie Croft

Liv and Val jog up
to the hut.

"Liv! Sit on the big log,"
said Val.

Liv and Val sat on the log.

"Look! Bugs!" said Val.

"This bug is red!" said Val.

The bug ran up the big log.

It ran up Val's leg!

Val looks at the red bug.

It has lots of dots!

"I can see dots
on the bug," said Val.

"I can see bugs
on my leg!" said Liv.

"Lots of dots on bugs,"
said Val.
"And lots of bugs on us!"

CHECKING FOR MEANING

1. What colour was the first bug that Val found? *(Literal)*

2. Whose leg did the bug run up? *(Literal)*

3. What do you think Liv and Val were doing when they found the bugs? *(Inferential)*

EXTENDING VOCABULARY

bugs	Explain what a *bug* is. What other word could you use for *bugs*?
log	Look at the word *log*. How many sounds are in the word? Can you find another word in the book that rhymes with *log*?
lots and **dots**	How are the words *lots* and *dots* the same? What is different about them? What other words do you know that rhyme with *lots* and *dots*?

MOVING BEYOND THE TEXT

1. What would you do if there was a bug on your leg?

2. What other animals or things can you think of that have dots?

3. What might Liv and Val do when they get up from the log?

4. Which page of the book was your favourite? Why?

SPEED SOUNDS

Kk	Ll	Vv	Qq	Ww
Dd	Jj	Oo	Gg	Uu
Cc	Bb	Rr	Ee	Ff	Hh	Nn
Mm	Ss	Aa	Pp	Ii	Tt

PRACTICE WORDS

Val

log

Liv

leg

lots

Lots